# Dinosaurs in Action

Unearth the secrets behind dinosaur fossils

QEB Publishing

Rupert Matthews

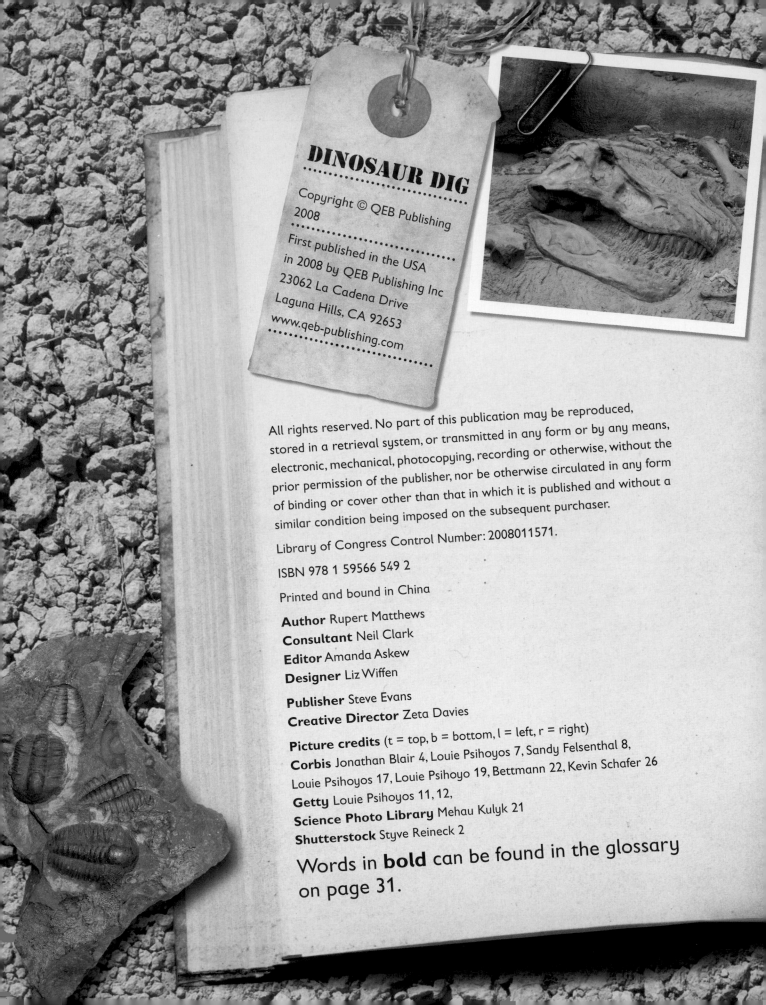

# DINOSAUR DIG

Copyright © QEB Publishing 2008

First published in the USA in 2008 by QEB Publishing Inc
23062 La Cadena Drive
Laguna Hills, CA 92653
www.qeb-publishing.com

Library of Congress Control Number: 2008011571.

ISBN 978 1 59566 549 2

Printed and bound in China

**Author** Rupert Matthews
**Consultant** Neil Clark
**Editor** Amanda Askew
**Designer** Liz Wiffen

**Publisher** Steve Evans
**Creative Director** Zeta Davies

**Picture credits** (t = top, b = bottom, l = left, r = right)
**Corbis** Jonathan Blair 4, Louie Psihoyos 7, Sandy Felsenthal 8, Louie Psihoyos 17, Louie Psihoyo 19, Bettmann 22, Kevin Schafer 26
**Getty** Louie Psihoyos 11, 12,
**Science Photo Library** Mehau Kulyk 21
**Shutterstock** Styve Reineck 2

Words in **bold** can be found in the glossary on page 31.

# CONTENTS

DINOSAUR DIG .................................................. 4

DINOSAUR RUNNERS ........................................ 6

STRIPPING LEAVES ........................................... 8

THE SOUND OF FOOD ..................................... 10

EXPLORING THE AIR ........................................ 12

HIBERNATION .................................................. 14

INTO THE FUTURE ........................................... 16

ON THE SCENT ................................................ 18

A TASTY SNACK ............................................... 20

A GAME OF BLUFF .......................................... 22

ALARM! ............................................................ 24

FINAL BATTLE ................................................. 26

DINO GUIDE

For every dinosaur in this book and many more, learn how to pronounce their name, find out their length and weight, and discover what they ate.

TRIASSIC PERIOD ............................................ 28

JURASSIC PERIOD ........................................... 29

CRETACEOUS PERIOD ..................................... 30

GLOSSARY 31

INDEX 32

# DINOSAUR DIG

Dinosaurs **were a group of** reptiles **that lived on Earth millions of years ago.**

There were many different types of dinosaur. Some dinosaurs had feathers or were brightly colored. The legs of modern reptiles, such as lizards, stick out sideways. Dinosaurs, however, had legs that were tucked under their body.

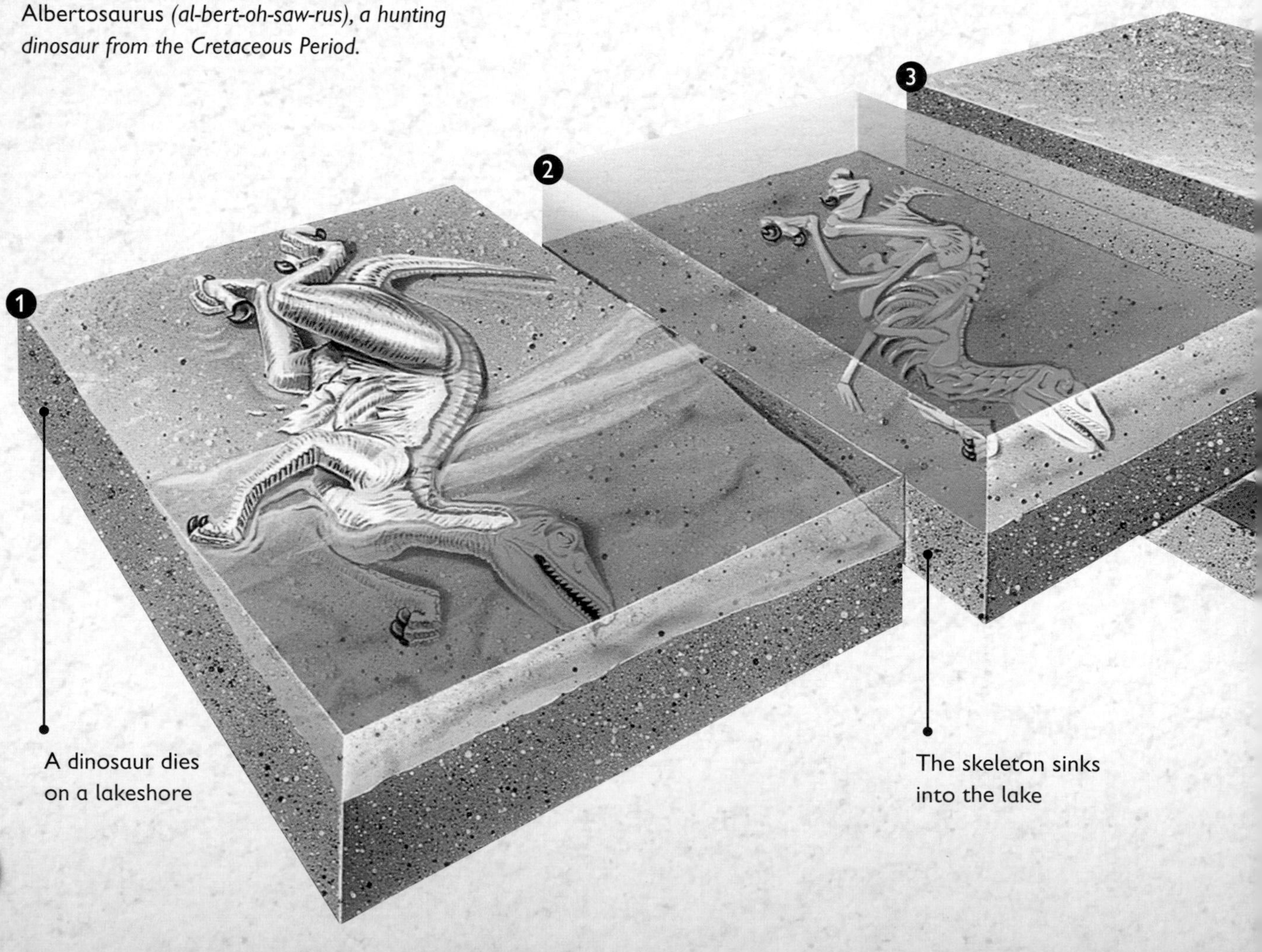

◐ A **paleontologist** (pay-lee-on-toll-oh-jist) excavates, or digs up, the **skull** and **skeleton** of Albertosaurus (al-bert-oh-saw-rus), a hunting dinosaur from the Cretaceous Period.

1

A dinosaur dies on a lakeshore

2

3

The skeleton sinks into the lake

Some dinosaurs could run quickly, or leap and jump. Others walked slowly with heavy steps. Some dinosaurs had sharp teeth and claws to attack their prey. A few dinosaurs had growths on their head, back, or sides. All dinosaurs were alert, active reptiles.

*⬤When a plant or animal dies, it usually rots away completely. However, in special conditions, parts of it can become fossilized.*

### How big were dinosaurs?

Every dinosaur is compared to an average adult, about 5 feet 2 in height, to show just how big they really were.

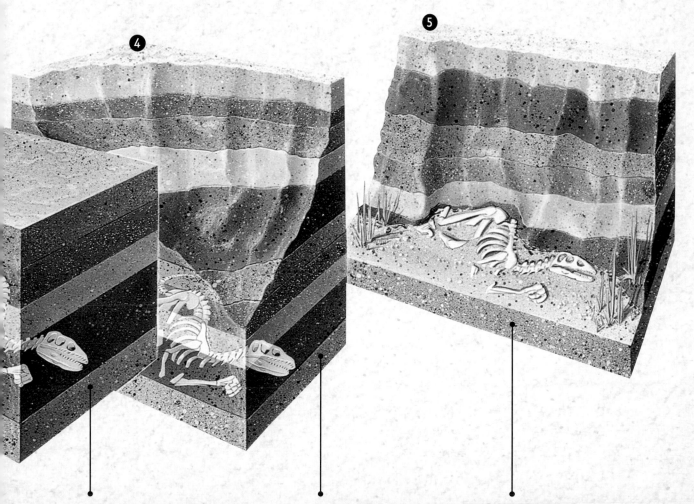

Layers of mud settle over the skeleton. The mud and bones gradually turn into stone

The rock wears away, or **erodes**

As more rock erodes, the skeleton is revealed

# DINOSAUR RUNNERS

**Dinosaurs could run well. This skill was important for chasing prey and escaping from danger.**

**DIG SITE**

As their legs grew straight down from the hips, dinosaurs only needed to move their legs in order to walk or run. Other reptiles need to swing their body from side to side because their legs grow out from the sides. Therefore, dinosaurs could move faster while using less energy than many other reptiles.

*Coelophysis* (see-low-fye-sis) was an early hunting dinosaur. It ran on its back legs. *Coelophysis* was fast and agile enough to snap up other smaller animals of the time. It was also able to flee quickly from danger.

## WOW!

There are two dinosaur groups. The ornithischians had hips like modern birds, and the saurischians had hips like modern lizards.

◗ *Dinosaurs and other animals flee as fire sweeps across the Triassic landscape of North America. Events such as this have been recorded in the fossil record —a list of all the fossils ever discovered.*

◖ A *fossil* skeleton of Coelophysis. The remains of its last meal have been preserved inside its stomach.

**Coelophysis**

10 feet in length

# STRIPPING LEAVES

## DINOSAUR DIG
### Brachiosaurus

**WHERE:** Colorado, North America

**PERIOD:** 150 million years ago in the late Jurassic

**DIG SITE**

Sauropod **dinosaurs were the biggest dinosaurs of all, but they had the smallest mouths.**

The leaves and shoots that sauropods ate did not give much energy. As they were so big, sauropods needed to eat huge amounts every day to survive.

It is thought that sauropods did not chew their food at all. They bit off a mouthful of leaves and swallowed them immediately. Sauropods swallowed stones that were moved about by the stomach muscles to mash up the leaves and twigs.

◑ *A fossilized skull of Brachiosaurus (brack-ee-oh-saw-rus). The large openings in the skull are for the eyes and nostrils. The huge nostrils may have contained veins carrying blood that could be cooled by the air as it was breathed in.*

# WOW!

Sauropods had such a long neck that food did not arrive in their stomach until 30 seconds after they swallowed it.

Brachiosaurus *prepares to take a mouthful of leaves from a tree. Its long neck allowed Brachiosaurus to eat food that other dinosaurs could not reach.*

**Brachiosaurus**

80 feet in length

# THE SOUND OF FOOD

Animals rely on their sense of hearing, especially if they live in dense forests where it is difficult to see for more than a few feet.

Hunters listen out for prey, and plant eaters try to hear if a hunter is nearby. Dinosaur ears were fairly simple. It is thought that they did not have ear flaps. There was probably just a simple hole leading to the ear mechanism.

DIG SITE

## WOW!

If a dinosaur put its jaws on the ground, it could "hear" vibrations made by the footsteps of nearby animals.

◖ Allosaurus *(al-oh-saw-rus)* stops to listen to a sound—it may be prey nearby. Hearing is a key sense for hunting animals and may make the difference between a successful hunt and hunger.

◗ *A fossilized skeleton of Allosaurus. The large, powerful head and strong claws on the front limbs show it was an active hunter.*

*Allosaurus* was a large hunter that probably preyed on sauropods, preferring to attack old or weak individuals as they would be easier to kill.

**Allosaurus**

40 feet in length

# EXPLORING THE AIR

*Microraptor* (my-krow-rap-tor), meaning "tiny hunter," was named by the scientist who found it because it looked like a small hunting dinosaur.

Then it was noticed that the dinosaur had feathers growing from its arms, legs, and tail. The feathers were long and strong, like those of a modern bird wing. However, its muscles were not strong enough to enable it to fly.

## DINOSAUR DIG
### Microraptor

**WHERE:** Liaoning, China, Asia

**PERIOD:** 130 million years ago in the early Cretaceous

**DIG SITE**

◖A *Microraptor* fossil preserved in rock. The feathers can be clearly seen around the bones. Delicate features, such as feathers, are rarely preserved.

It is now thought that *Microraptor* used its feathers to glide for short distances. It may have lived in forests where it climbed trees to look for insects to feed on. The tail was probably used to control steering in the air.

⬤ *Microraptor probably glided from one tree to the next to escape from danger or to pounce on food.*

**Microraptor**

2 feet in length

## WOW!

In 1999, a man glued the front end of a *Microraptor* fossil to the back end of a different dinosaur fossil. He then pretended that he had found a new type of dinosaur, but the truth was soon revealed.

# HIBERNATION

**Although the Earth was warmer and wetter during the time of the dinosaurs, there were areas with cooler weather.**

Australia and New Zealand lay close to the South Pole about 110 million years ago. During winter, the sun did not shine for weeks on end. The weather was very cold and no plants could grow.

Some of the larger dinosaurs may have walked to warmer areas in winter, but smaller dinosaurs could not escape. Instead, they hibernated.

When an animal hibernates it goes into a very deep sleep. The heart rate and breathing slow down, the body temperature drops, and all bodily functions become slower. During this time, the creature survives on fat stored in its body.

## DINOSAUR DIG
Leaellynasaura
Timimus

**WHERE:** Southern Australia

**PERIOD:** 106 million years ago in the early Cretaceous

DIG SITE

## WOW!

Scientists did not know that dinosaurs lived in cold parts of the world until the fossil of *Leaellynasaura* was found in Australia in the late 1900s.

◗ *A scene from Australia about 106 million years ago. The larger dinosaur Timimus (tim-ee-mus) hibernates under a log while a group of smaller Leaellynasaura (lee-ell-in-ah-saw-rah) look up at the Southern Lights.*

**Leaellynasaura**

6.5 feet in length

**Timimus**

11 feet in length

# INTO THE FUTURE

Paleontologists believe that birds come from small hunting dinosaurs. They both have feathers, walk on their back legs, and have hollow limb bones.

Some scientists think that the two groups are so similar that they should belong to a single group. They believe that dinosaurs did not become **extinct**, they just became birds instead.

**DINOSAUR DIG**
**Archaeopteryx**
.......................................
**WHERE:** Southern Germany, Europe
.......................................
**PERIOD:** 155 million years ago in the late Jurassic
.......................................

**DIG SITE**

Other scientists point out the differences between the groups. Dinosaurs had teeth, birds do not. Birds can fly, most dinosaurs could not. These scientists think that dinosaurs and birds should continue to be seen as different groups of animals.

## WOW!

Some scientists think that birds come from a particular family of dinosaurs called the tetanurans, which later **evolved** into the tyrannosaurs.

◐ This fossilized Archaeopteryx (ark-ee-op-tur-iks) shows the feathers and how they are arranged to form two wings. When this fossil was found, it showed a link between dinosaurs and birds.

**Archaeopteryx**

1.5 feet in length

◐ Archaeopteryx perches on a tree branch. Scientists think that Archaeopteryx was a good flyer, but only over short distances.

# ON THE SCENT

The sense of smell is important to most animals. Plant eaters can smell a hunter from some distance away and may flee before it becomes a danger.

Hunters use scent to track down prey. Also, if the wind is blowing away from the hunter, their victim will not be able to smell them approaching.

The parts of the nose that are used to smell are never fossilized. Therefore, scientists cannot be certain how well dinosaurs could smell. However, some species have long, twisted nostrils as if they contained scent receptors, so these dinosaurs could probably smell better than others.

## DINOSAUR DIG
### Velociraptor
**WHERE:** Mongolia, Asia

**WHEN:** 75 million years ago in the late Cretaceous

DIG SITE

◗ A **pack** of Velociraptor (vel-oss-ee-rap-tor) moves through a Cretaceous forest. There is some evidence that these dinosaurs hunted as a group, working together to find and overcome prey.

⊖ This fossilized skull of a Velociraptor shows that this dinosaur had around 80 sharp, curved teeth set in long narrow jaws. This was ideal for eating meat once prey had been killed.

Velociraptor

6.5 feet in length

# A TASTY SNACK

**It is usually thought that larger hunters preyed on large plant eaters.**

However, even the biggest hunter would have snapped up a much smaller animal if it got the chance. A baby dinosaur or other small creature would have been killed instantly by one bite of the giant jaws.

Scientists think that the big hunters had such strong chemicals in their stomach that they may have been able to digest the bones. Others think that the bones were regurgitated from the stomach once the meat had been digested.

DINOSAUR DIG
**Tarbosaurus**
WHERE: Mongolia, Asia
WHEN: 70 million years ago in the late Cretaceous

DIG SITE

## WOW!

*Tarbosaurus* lived in Asia and *Tyrannosaurus* (tie-rann-oh-saw-rus) in America, but they were very similar. Some scientists believe they were the same animal.

◗ The hunter Tarbosaurus (tar-bow-saw-rus) prepares to snap up a young hadrosaur dinosaur. Its long, stabbing teeth and powerful jaws would kill such a small animal with a single bite.

*Tarbosaurus* was a tyrannosaur that grew to be about 40 feet in length. Like other tyrannosaurs, it had very powerful jaws, but tiny front claws. Some scientists think that *Tarbosaurus* could not tackle large dinosaurs, so it fed on smaller animals or **carrion**.

⬤ The fossilized head and neck of Tarbosaurus show that this dinosaur had a deep snout and jaws attached to very powerful muscles. Its bite was probably strong enough to crush bones.

Tarbosaurus

40 feet in length

# A GAME OF BLUFF

When they meet a dangerous hunter or rival, many animals will try to make themselves look bigger and stronger than they really are. They hope that this will **frighten** off the other animal.

Many scientists think that **ceratopian** dinosaurs used their **neck frill** as a **bluffing** weapon. The frill looked large and impressive. The animal would lift up its frill so that it looked as big as possible, then move it from side to side. It was actually made of a thin layer of bone and skin. The frill may also have been used to attract females before mating.

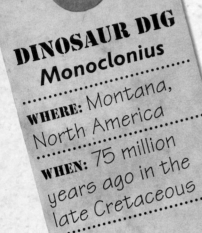

## DINOSAUR DIG
### Monoclonius

**WHERE:** Montana, North America

**WHEN:** 75 million years ago in the late Cretaceous

DIG SITE

◐ *A rare complete skeleton of* Monoclonius *(mon-oh-clone-ee-us). Usually only part of the skeleton is found. A skeleton such as this allows scientists to see how the complete animal appeared.*

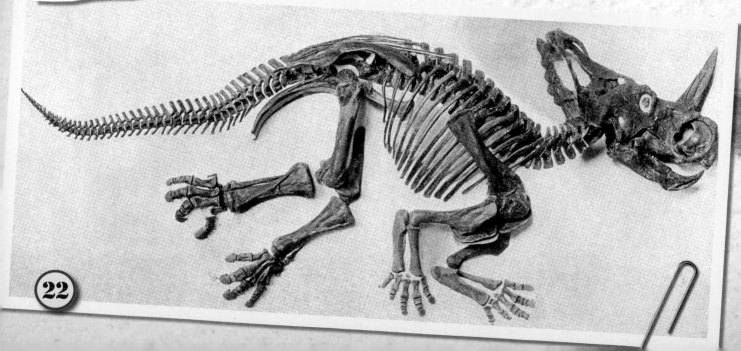

## WOW!

The dinosaur *Centrosaurus* (sen-tro-saw-rus) was identical to *Monoclonius*, except that its horn curved forward slightly instead of backward.

**Monoclonius**

16.5 feet in length

⬤ *Monoclonius lowers its head and stamps on the ground with its front feet as it prepares for a fight. Combats may have been between rivals of the same species, or against hunters.*

# ALARM!

**Plant eaters that live in herds or flocks usually have a way of warning others if danger threatens.**

Some animals will call loudly or stamp their feet on the ground to make a noise. Others have brightly colored parts of their body that they will reveal suddenly, flashing a patch of color on and off.

## DINOSAUR DIG

Anserimimus
Oviraptor
Protoceratops
Tarbosaurus

**WHERE:** Mongolia, Asia

**WHEN:** 75 million years ago in the late Cretaceous

**DIG SITE**

### Protoceratops

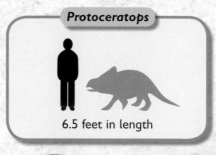

6.5 feet in length

A pair of Protoceratops (pro-toe-ser-ah-tops) guard their nest.

### Oviraptor

6.5 feet in length

Some dinosaurs had brightly colored feathers growing from their tail. These may have been used as an alarm signal. The dinosaur would show the back of the fan as it fled from danger. Other dinosaurs would follow because they knew that they would also be running away from the hunting dinosaur.

A tyrannosaur chases Anserimimus (ann-sair-ee-me-mus) and Oviraptor (oh-vee-rap-tor).

**Anserimimus**

10 feet in length

**Tarbosaurus**

40 feet in length

# FINAL BATTLE

**As conditions changed, new types of dinosaur gradually evolved and older types died out.**

Sauropods became much rarer and stegosaurs died out completely. They were replaced by ceratopians and hadrosaurs.

Suddenly, about 65 million years ago, all the dinosaurs became extinct. Many other types of animal died out at the same time.

Scientists are not certain what caused this mass extinction. Some think that a meteorite hit the Earth, wiping out huge numbers of animals. Others think that a sudden change in climate caused the deaths.

**DINOSAUR DIG**

Triceratops

Tyrannosaurus

**WHERE:** Colorado, North America

**WHEN:** 65 million years ago in the late Cretaceous

**DIG SITE**

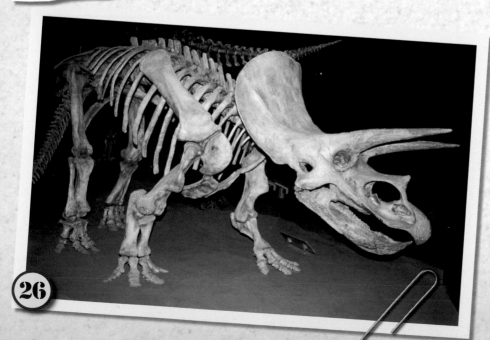

◖ This skeleton of Triceratops (try-ser-ah-tops) shows both the long, sharp horns and the large neck frill. It was a sturdy, powerful animal.

◉ Triceratops *prepares to face* Tyrannosaurus *(tie-rann-oh-saw-rus) in battle.* Tyrannosaurus *would have tried to avoid the sharp horns of its prey.*

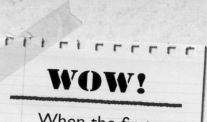

# WOW!

When the first dinosaur fossils were found, people thought that they were the bones of giant men.

*Tyrannosaurus*

40 feet in length

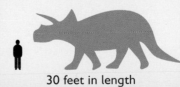

*Triceratops*

30 feet in length

# DINO GUIDE

## Coelophysis (p6)
**PRONUNCIATION**
see-low-fye-sis
**LENGTH** 10 feet
**WEIGHT** 75–80 pounds
**DIET** Small animals

## Plateosaurus
**PRONUNCIATION**
plat-ee-oh-saw-rus
**LENGTH** 26 feet
**WEIGHT** 1 ton
**DIET** Plants

## Efraasia
**PRONUNCIATION**
ef-rah-see-ah
**LENGTH** 23 feet
**WEIGHT** 1,300 pounds
**DIET** Plants

## Procompsognathus
**PRONUNCIATION**
pro-comp-sog-nay-thus
**LENGTH** 4 feet
**WEIGHT** 4.5–6.5 pounds
**DIET** Small animals

## Eoraptor
**PRONUNCIATION**
ee-oh-rap-tor
**LENGTH** 3 feet
**WEIGHT** 7–30 pounds
**DIET** Small animals

## Riojasaurus
**PRONUNCIATION**
ree-oh-ha-saw-rus
**LENGTH** 33 feet
**WEIGHT** 1 ton
**DIET** Plants

## Herrerasaurus
**PRONUNCIATION**
he-ray-ra-saw-rus
**LENGTH** 10 feet
**WEIGHT** 450 pounds
**DIET** Animals

## Saltopus
**PRONUNCIATION**
sall-toe-puss
**LENGTH** Less than 3 feet
**WEIGHT** 2–4.5 pounds
**DIET** Small animals

## Pisanosaurus
**PRONUNCIATION**
peez-an-oh-saw-rus
**LENGTH** 3 feet
**WEIGHT** 6.5 pounds
**DIET** Plants

## Staurikosaurus
**PRONUNCIATION**
store-ick-oh-saw-rus
**LENGTH** 6.5 feet
**WEIGHT** 65 pounds
**DIET** Small animals

# JURASSIC PERIOD
## 206 TO 145 MILLION YEARS AGO

### Allosaurus (p10)
**PRONUNCIATION**
al-oh-saw-rus
**LENGTH** 40 feet
**WEIGHT** 1.5–2 tons
**DIET** Animals

### Apatosaurus
**PRONUNCIATION**
ap-at-oh-saw-rus
**LENGTH** 80 feet
**WEIGHT** 25–35 tons
**DIET** Plants

### Archaeopteryx (p16)
**PRONUNCIATION**
ark-ee-op-tur-iks
**LENGTH** 1.5 feet
**WEIGHT** 1 pound
**DIET** Animals

### Brachiosaurus (p8)
**PRONUNCIATION**
brack-ee-oh-saw-rus
**LENGTH** 80 feet
**WEIGHT** 50 tons
**DIET** Plants

### Camptosaurus
**PRONUNCIATION**
kamp-toe-saw-rus
**LENGTH** 20 feet
**WEIGHT** 1–2 tons
**DIET** Plants

### Cetiosaurus
**PRONUNCIATION**
set-ee-oh-saw-rus
**LENGTH** 60 feet
**WEIGHT** 15–20 tons
**DIET** Plants

### Compsognathus
**PRONUNCIATION**
comp-sog-nay-thus
**LENGTH** 3–5 feet
**WEIGHT** 6.5 pounds
**DIET** Small animals

### Dicraeosaurus
**PRONUNCIATION**
die-kree-oh-saw-rus
**LENGTH** 43–65 feet
**WEIGHT** 10 tons
**DIET** Plants

### Kentrosaurus
**PRONUNCIATION**
ken-troe-saw-rus
**LENGTH** 16.5 feet
**WEIGHT** 2 tons
**DIET** Plants

### Megalosaurus
**PRONUNCIATION**
meg-ah-low-saw-rus
**LENGTH** 30 feet
**WEIGHT** 1 ton
**DIET** Plants

# CRETACEOUS PERIOD
## 145 TO 65 MILLION YEARS AGO

### Albertosaurus (p4)
**PRONUNCIATION**
al-bert-oh-saw-rus
**LENGTH** 30 feet
**WEIGHT** 2.5 tons
**DIET** Animals

### Oviraptor (p24)
**PRONUNCIATION**
oh-vee-rap-tor
**LENGTH** 6.5 feet
**WEIGHT** 65 pounds
**DIET** Small animals and plants

### Anserimimus (p24)
**PRONUNCIATION**
ann-sair-ee-me-mus
**LENGTH** 10 feet
**WEIGHT** 650 pounds
**DIET** Small animals

### Protoceratops (p24)
**PRONUNCIATION**
pro-toe-ser-ah-tops
**LENGTH** 6.5 feet
**WEIGHT** 330–550 pounds
**DIET** Plants

### Centrosaurus (p23)
**PRONUNCIATION**
sen-tro-saw-rus
**LENGTH** 20 feet
**WEIGHT** 3 tons
**DIET** Plants

### Tarbosaurus (p20 and 24)
**PRONUNCIATION**
tar-bow-saw-rus
**LENGTH** 40 feet
**WEIGHT** 4 tons
**DIET** Large animals

### Leaellynasaura (p14)
**PRONUNCIATION**
lee-ell-in-ah-saw-rah
**LENGTH** 6.5 feet
**WEIGHT** 22 pounds
**DIET** Plants

### Timimus (p14)
**PRONUNCIATION**
tim-ee-mus
**LENGTH** 11 feet
**WEIGHT** 650 pounds
**DIET** Unknown

### Microraptor (p12)
**PRONUNCIATION**
my-krow-rap-tor
**LENGTH** 2 feet
**WEIGHT** 2 pounds
**DIET** Small animals

### Triceratops (p26)
**PRONUNCIATION**
try-ser-ah-tops
**LENGTH** 30 feet
**WEIGHT** 5–8 tons
**DIET** Plants

### Monoclonius (p22)
**PRONUNCIATION**
mon-oh-clone-ee-us
**LENGTH** 16.5 feet
**WEIGHT** 2–3 tons
**DIET** Plants

**Tyrannosaurus** (p20 and 27)
**PRONUNCIATION**
tie-rann-oh-saw-rus
**LENGTH** 40 feet
**WEIGHT** 6 tons
**DIET** Large animals

**Velociraptor** (p18)
**PRONUNCIATION**
vel-oss-ee-rap-tor
**LENGTH** 6.5 feet
**WEIGHT** 45–65 pounds
**DIET** Small animals

# GLOSSARY

**Bluff** To deceive someone by pretending to be someone else.

**Carrion** Meat from a dead animal that the hunter has not killed itself.

**Ceratopian** A group of dinosaurs that had a neck frill and teeth designed for slicing. Most ceratopians also had horns on their head.

**Cretaceous** The third period of time in the age of the dinosaurs. The Cretaceous began about 145 million years ago and ended about 65 million years ago.

**Dinosaur** A type of reptile that lived millions of years ago. All dinosaurs are now extinct.

**Erode** To wear away.

**Extinct** Not existing any more. An animal is extinct when they have all died out.

**Evolve** To develop gradually over a long period of time.

**Fossil** Any part of a plant or animal that has been preserved in rock. Also traces of plants or animals, such as footprints.

**Jurassic** The second period of time in the age of the dinosaurs. The Jurassic began about 206 million years ago and ended about 145 million years ago.

**Neck frill** A thin plate of bone and skin growing from the back of an animal's skull.

**Pack** A group of hunting animals.

**Paleontologist** A scientist who studies ancient forms of life, including dinosaurs.

**Regurgitate** To bring swallowed food up from the stomach into the mouth.

**Reptile** A cold-blooded animal, such as a lizard. Dinosaurs were reptiles, too.

**Sauropod** A type of dinosaur that had a long neck and tail. Sauropods included the largest of all dinosaurs.

**Skeleton** The bones in an animal's body.

**Skull** The bones of the head of an animal. The skull does not include the jaw, but many skulls have jaws attached.

**Triassic** The first period of time in the age of the dinosaurs. The Triassic began about 248 million years ago and ended about 208 million years ago.

# INDEX

Albertosaurus 4, 30
Allosaurus 10, 11, 29
Anserimimus 24, 25, 30
Apatosaurus 29
Archaeopteryx 16, 17, 29

birds 16
body temperature 14
Brachiosaurus 8, 9, 29

Camptosaurus 29
carrion 21, 31
Centrosaurus 23, 30
ceratopians 22, 26, 31
Cetiosaurus 29
climate 26
Coelophysis 6, 7, 28
Compsognathus 29

Dicraeosaurus 29
digestion 20

Efraasia 28
Eoraptor 28
evolution 16, 26, 31
extinction 16, 26, 31

feathers 4, 12, 13, 16,
    17, 25
fossils 5, 6, 7, 8, 11, 12, 13,
    14, 17, 18, 19, 21,
    17, 31,

hadrosaurs 20, 26
hearing 10
herds 24
Herrerasaurus 28
hibernation 14
hips 6
horns 23, 26, 27

Kentrosaurus 29

Leaellynasaura 14, 30

Megalosaurus 29
Microraptor 12, 13, 30
Monoclonius 22, 30

neck frills 22, 26, 31
nests 24

ornithischians 6
Oviraptor 24, 25, 30

packs 18, 25, 31
paleontologist 4, 16, 31
Pisanosaurus 28
Plateosaurus 28
Procompsognathus 28
Protoceratops 24, 30

Riojasaurus 28

Saltopus 28
saurischians 6
sauropods 8, 9, 11, 26, 31
senses 10, 18
South Pole 14
Staurikosaurus 28
stegosaurs 26
stomach 7, 8, 9, 20

Tarbosaurus 20, 21, 24,
    25, 30
tetanurans 16
Timimus 14, 30
Triceratops 26, 27, 30
tyrannosaurs 16, 21, 25
Tyrannosaurus 20, 26, 27,
    30

Velociraptor 18, 19, 30